IN THE PRESENCE OF GOD

Devotions
for the
Newly Married

with the expectation
that a few moments
of quiet reflection
together each day
will heighten your delight
in a life together.

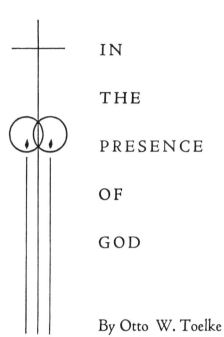

IN

THE

PRESENCE

OF

GOD

By Otto W. Toelke

CONCORDIA PUBLISHING HOUSE, ST. LOUIS

Sixth Printing 1965

Concordia Publishing House, Saint Louis 18, Missouri
Concordia Publishing House Ltd., London, E. C. 1.
Copyright 1962 by Concordia Publishing House
Library of Congress Catalog Card No. 61-18225

Manufactured in the United States of America

FOREWORD

Nowhere is the general brittleness of our modern world more evident than in the marriage relationship. Here we have a great proof that ours is a neurotic and anxious age. It is inevitable that one of the most delicate and sensitive relationships in human life should be profoundly touched by the instability of our world. The author of these very relevant devotions for young married people says very properly: "It was only about a century ago — the era of our great-grandparents — when the problems associated with marriage, the family, and the home were given very little attention. They did not require the extensive study and investigation they are receiving today. Society was not nearly as complex as it is today. The economic role, the social status, the physical responsibility, and the division of labor for husband and wife were all quite clearly defined as compared with the mixed and clouded thinking that we have on these matters today."

The church has a major interest in marriage for two reasons. There is, first of all, the task of bringing God's imperatives to bear upon the problems of matrimony. The lives of men and women must be brought under the gentle yoke of the Gospel. This is a difficult and unceasing task. It is only through the Word of God that we can expect a successful transition from the excessive romanticism of our day to the deep, quiet, unspectacular love and companionship of the long years of marriage. This is, after all, the ultimate test, and the author of these devotions has seen the decisiveness of this transition with thoughtful wisdom.

The second reason for the church's interest in marriage is that, humanly speaking, the individual parish is dependent on stable family units to furnish the social foundations for a happy and well-organized congregational life. This is exceedingly important. It is not only nostalgia which causes us to look back on the old days of the family pew with father and mother and the children ranged like organ pipes. Behind this nostalgia is the realization that this was part of the strength and joy of the church. It was a certain and complete assurance of a splendid present and a great future. The church's reasons for her interest in matrimony are therefore theological, social, and practical.

In an inspired moment the author decided to base his devotions on the beautiful phrases of the marriage ceremony. This ceremony is largely common to all churches in the Protestant tradition, and for that reason also this volume should have a wide circulation. If these devotions are used faithfully, the magnificent phrases of the liturgy will become a part of the warp and woof of marriage and a constant reminder of the sacred beauty of the marital relationship.

The author brings to his task not only a rich and thoughtful parish experience but also years of special study of the problems connected with married life. For a number of years I have had the privilege of observing his work in a parish in which very many young people were members. My personal observation is that his counseling was always both theologically and psychologically sound. Hundreds of young people, also on the campus of Valparaiso University, have benefited from his wise and thoughtful guidance.

I hope that in one way or another this little volume will come into the hands of all young married couples who have stood before the altars in our church. I hope, too, that pastors will give it as a wedding gift to the young people whom they unite and bless. It will always bring a lingering echo of the beauty and splendor of the marriage liturgy.

When a young man and woman stand before the altar of God, we see that two hands are joined together. However, their marriage will be fine and holy only if we remember that a third hand is also there, invisible and once torn by nails, but powerful and gracious, to bring happiness to two human souls. This the author has tried to demonstrate and illustrate — and he has succeeded remarkably well.

O. P. KRETZMANN

The Day of St. Michael
and All Angels, 1961

PREFACE

This little volume requires some explanation. It is intended for a very specific group — the newly-married. The twenty-eight devotions are based on phrases taken from the marriage ritual. Ideally, use of the devotions should begin during the honeymoon, when the words of the ritual are more likely to be remembered and to strike a responsive chord.

If the devotions are not as devout and worshipfully spiritual as they might be, it is not only because of a lack of ability on the part of the writer; it is because they are intended to get the newly-married couple started in the practice of family devotions rather than to lift them up beyond the stars. There is an old German maxim which, loosely translated, says "a good beginning is half the victory." If the newly-married couple begin their marriage by regularly and freely speaking to each other about the things of God and of the spirit, this is, indeed, good and augurs well for the future of the marriage.

If acknowledgements for motivation to write these devotions were to be recorded, we would have to place at the top of the list the hundreds of young couples we were privileged to serve as a marital counselor during eighteen years in the parish ministry.

The undersigned sends forth this little volume with an honest and deep sense of its many shortcomings but with the sincere prayer that it will help bring to some the blessing that the bride and groom at the wedding of Cana enjoyed more than 1900 years ago. Christ was a guest in their home from its very beginning.

OTTO W. TOELKE

September 28, 1961
Valparaiso, Indiana

The beautiful and impressive words of the marriage ritual, "We are assembled here in the presence of God and these witnesses to join together this man and this woman in holy matrimony . . ." still ring in your ears. It has been only a matter of hours since the pastor intoned the words that announced to God and the world that from this day forward you will live as one person. You will not only share with each other, but you will give to each other all that it is possible for you to give of love, of spirit, and of understanding.

It was a beautiful ceremony. It was almost like magic. You entered the church unmarried, and then, within a matter of minutes, everything in your lives suddenly changed. Before, there were two hearts, two minds, two spirits. Then, suddenly, as you left the church, it was — and this is not as unreal as it may sound — one heart, one mind, and one spirit. Never, as long as either shall live, can your thoughts about the things that really matter in life exclude the welfare of the other.

The union of husband and wife is close and intimate. Indeed, it is one of the strongest of human bonds. It was designed by the heavenly Architect. You entered this union, as the ritual says, "in the presence of God." You need never be frightened and the union will never be threatened or broken as long as you remain in the presence of God.

Our Savior Jesus Christ, who gave Himself into death for our sins and rose again victoriously from that death, has given us the blessed assurance that His presence is available to us at all times. In His holy Word He tells us, "Lo, I am with you alway, even unto the end of the world."

If the presence of God is lost, it is not because He withdraws from us, but because we, by our sins, withdraw from Him. Your marriage was sealed in the presence of God. He wanted it that way. You wanted it that way. Resolve in these first days of your marriage that, with His help, you will do everything to keep it in the presence of God.

PRAYER

Dear Savior, in whom we live and move and have our being, and without whom we can do nothing, keep us always, we pray Thee, in Thy loving presence. As we began our marriage before Thy holy altar, so bless this union to Thy glory and our good, that someday, hand in hand, we will know the fullness of joy that is at Thy right hand. Amen.

Have you ever tried to explain the origin of marriage apart from God? It is a most difficult thing to do. Modern anthropologists and sociologists, studying the origin and development of man and society, glibly write that the male and the female were driven together by sheer biological impulse or necessity, or by the herding instinct; that there were certain animal passions or drives in both male and female, and seeing themselves as physically complementing each other, they were naturally drawn together.

One man of God once made the statement that when we attempt to explain the origin of marriage in this particular way we soon find ourselves using the language of the barnyard. Such an explanation, the one apart from God, tends to degrade man and marriage.

Is it not much more credible and beautiful to take the Holy Record as we find it in the very first book of the Bible (Genesis 2:18, 21-24): "And the Lord God said, It is not good that the man should be alone; I will make him an help meet for him. . . . And the Lord God caused a deep sleep to fall upon Adam, and he slept: and He took one of his ribs and closed up the flesh instead thereof; and the rib which the Lord God had taken from man made He a woman, and brought her unto the man. And Adam said, This is now bone of my bones and flesh of my flesh; she shall be called Woman, because she was taken out of man. Therefore shall a man leave his father and his mother and shall cleave unto his wife; and they shall be one flesh."

This simple but mysterious, this beautiful and profound record of the origin of marriage is the one the Christian accepts. He not only accepts it, but clings to it. The Bible record makes him think of himself and his spouse as children of God rather than brutes or animals. Secondly, the Bible record puts into marriage not only the purpose of propagation, but the high and noble purposes of the divine order. Thirdly, the Bible record is no more fraught with difficulties than other explanations of the origin of marriage.

Some may say that they do not leave God out of the picture, but that they cannot believe that He operated so directly in the lives of men. They have forgotten that He did so when He Himself became man, came down to earth in the form of the Savior Christ, and suffered and died for the sins of the world. And someday He will claim as His own all who believe this.

Lord God, heavenly Father, Creator and Redeemer of all, we are the creatures of Thy word and the work of Thy hands. Even as Thou hast created us, Thou hast ordained that we live together as man and wife. May the relationship of our marriage always be high and holy as Thou didst intend it when bringing the first woman to the first man. We ask it in Jesus' name. Amen.

Have you ever taken the time to page through the dictionary and look up the word "matrimony"? A good dictionary will tell you that in addition to the married state, or wedlock, the word matrimony can refer also to a game of cards and to the combination of a king and a queen in some games.

Modern humorists, with their satire and irony, could, of course, give us any number of definitions that are amusing but hardly enlightening or inspiring.

In the marriage rite which was used at your wedding the words "to join together this man and this woman in holy matrimony" were spoken. It is not absolutely necessary that you have a profound understanding of the word "matrimony" in order that your marriage be successful and God-pleasing, but it is all-important that you are aware of, and have a reasonable understanding of, the word that immediately precedes the word matrimony in the Christian marriage ritual. We, of course, mean the word "holy."

An offhand and rule-of-thumb definition for the word holy is — "without sin." Since you were united in *holy* matrimony, does this mean that your marriage is without sin? The answer is yes and no. No — your marriage is not holy, for neither your marriage nor any other marriage ever consummated on the face of the earth has been without sin. Since the components themselves, the man and the woman who go into marriage, are sinful, the whole that issues from the union must also be sinful. Yes — your marriage is holy, because it was instituted by the most high God, because the estate was blessed by Him, because it was performed in His presence, but most of all, it is holy because Jesus, the Son of God Himself, imputes, attributes, or ascribes to the husband and wife who believe in Him the holiness or righteousness that He so dearly earned on Calvary's cross.

The Bible clearly states, "all our righteousnesses are as filthy rags." More simply put, it means that without Christ there is no good in us. So also, without Christ your marriage can only be unholy matrimony. It becomes *holy* matrimony only when each marriage partner kneels in humble obedience before the Savior of all, confesses sins against both God and man, and receives forgiveness. This means that the sins have been removed, that a state of holiness in Christ exists. In this sense only can two people live in the estate of holy matrimony.

PRAYER

"Ye shall be holy, for I the Lord your God am holy." We know this, dear Lord, to be Thy command. Grant that in our marriage we will never seek this holiness in ourselves or in each other, where it can never be found. Give us rather the bended knee, the bowed head, and the humble heart so that we may gratefully wear the crown of holiness earned for us by Thy Son and our Savior, Jesus Christ. Amen.

When you, as Christians, chose each other as lifelong companions and partners in marriage, it was assumed that the choice was not made unadvisedly or lightly. Sometimes it is. There are those who regard marriage as a mere social arrangement. If the arrangement is not pleasing and satisfying, then, they feel, society furnishes them with an escape called divorce, and presto! the problem is solved.

However, even among those whose attitude is Christian and wholesome, there are times when holy matrimony is entered into unadvisedly or lightly. This comes about not by indifference, but rather by a lack of understanding of the many facets of human personality.

A nationally known marriage counselor put it this way: "Do you know that when you pick your life companion you are choosing a habit system, a cultural background, a set of loyalties, and a life philosophy? These should be understood and accepted."

Habits, culture, loyalties, and philosophy are things that are not easily or quickly changed or altered. Usually these are either good or bad attributes of an individual that have been molded in the crucible of heredity and environment over the years.

If your marriage partner's conduct or thinking at times seems irregular or unusual or even distasteful to you, perhaps it is so only in the light of your background. Also, you should remember that this works both ways.

Just because a culture — and "culture" is a broad and all-inclusive term which embodies everything from diet and dress to music and customs — is different from the one in which you were reared, that does not mean that it is inferior or no good.

Every individual is a product of the world he has known, the people with whom he associated, the economic conditions under which he existed, the recreation he enjoyed, and the religious influence under which he lived.

To the degree that you overlook or disregard these factors in your relationship with your spouse you could be entering the state of holy matrimony unadvisedly or lightly. Bear in mind that the fabric of your marriage was fashioned from a thousand sources.

PRAYER

Dear Savior, even as the blessed Gospel of the salvation which Thou hast secured for us in Thy resurrection transcends the differences of culture and customs, class and clan, so may our love as husband and wife rise above man-made divisions and differences so that it will always redound to Thy glory and our good. Amen.

". . . AND THE TWO SHALL BECOME ONE." Matthew 19:5

"Marriage is a fifty-fifty proposition." How many times have you heard people make that statement? Some make the statement in all seriousness, honestly believing that if the proposition is always borne in mind, then marriage is invulnerable; no matter how many pitfalls, it will survive them all.

If marriage is nothing more than a "fifty-fifty" relationship, then we may as well reduce the whole thing to a business contract. But God never intended marriage merely as a contract. Nowhere in Holy Scripture do we find a passage indicating that in marriage all property is to be jointly owned by husband and wife, or that all responsibility is to be equally shared, or that each spouse is to have the same amount of leisure time and recreation, or that there is to be a distinct division of labor, or no division of labor. Perhaps the reason the Bible never mentions these things is simply because the Creator thought of and described marriage in far more noble, intimate, and personal terms. He said, ". . . and the two shall become one." In the sight of God, and therefore in the sight of the Christian, marriage is far more a union than it is a contract. It is the blending and bonding together of two people, spiritually, emotionally, socially, and physically. A contract is an instrument that forces one to carry out the conditions of an agreement. Marriage is an instrument of God used to bring two people into the closest harmony that human beings can know.

If you ever permit yourselves to take marriage from the high plane on which God Himself placed it, then you are downgrading a divine union to an earthly association.

What it means to become "one" with someone else is very difficult to express in words. Jesus, our Savior, became "one" with man when He left His heavenly throne in the incarnation. In so doing He felt the hurt of humiliation, the pain of poverty, the degradation of deceit, the leaden load of loneliness, the sickness of sin, and the doom of death. He never complained that He was being pushed beyond the requirements of a "contract." He also felt, and made it possible for us to feel, the throbbing heart of a loving God.

God, in Christ, became "one" with man so that someday man might be at home in the presence of God.

When a Christian husband and wife "become one" they assuredly cannot do for each other what Christ has done for every sinner, but they can constantly point to what has been done by Christ. This cannot be brought about by contractual agreement. Only a union permeated with Christian love can make two people "one" in the way in which Christ speaks of it.

PRAYER

O Jesus, whom we adore in the mystery of Trinity in unity, we thank Thee for becoming "one" with man. In this union our sins became Thy sins and Thy victory became ours. Grant that our union in marriage may pattern itself in "oneness" after Thee. Amen.

"WHOM GOD HATH JOINED TOGETHER." Matthew 19:6

How do I love thee? Let me count the ways.
I love thee to the depth and breadth and height
My soul can reach, when feeling out of sight
For the ends of Being and ideal Grace.
I love thee to the level of every day's
Most quiet need, by sun and candle-light.
I love thee freely, as men strive for Right;
I love thee purely, as they turn from Praise.
I love thee with the passion put to use
In my old griefs, and with my childhood's faith.
I love thee with a love I seemed to lose
With my lost saints — I love thee with the breath,
Smiles, tears, of all my life! — and, if God choose,
I shall but love thee better after death.

You do not have to be a lettered and cultured individual to see the quiet beauty and feel the warm depth of Elizabeth Browning's words. She wrote the sonnet to her husband.

From this sonnet and other literary works that come down to us from this particular period in English literature, we may assume that people in that day believed in the theory of "personal affinity" — the

14

theory that two people were intended only for each other. If one of them married a person with whom he or she did not have this "personal affinity," the results could be only disappointing and tragic.

If we take seriously the lyrics of many of the popular songs of our day, we would have to assume that there are still many, many people who believe in the theory of "personal affinity." They may not say it in their own words, but they borrow the words of a song or express the thought that each man must have his maid and that each maid is specifically intended for a certain man. If, among all the people in the world, these two people do not find each other, and settle for someone else, a tragic mismatch takes place.

The whole idea makes wonderful material for the song writers and poets, but if we examine the situation we would have to admit that the theory is more romantic than factual.

Yet, if we recall the words from the marriage ritual, "whom God hath joined together," we Christians cannot but feel that we, as husband and wife, have been brought together by greater and more discerning forces than mere chance and accident. For the Christian the feeling is real and valid.

Because you are believing Christians, there were prayers uttered, vows exchanged, and blessings bestowed before your actual marriage. God was in the picture ever and always.

Even if you do not believe that you have a "personal affinity" for each other, you have expressed the belief that you each have a "personal affinity" in and for Christ. In Him, the Head, you are joined as members of the same body. This is a union that by far transcends any union expressed in poem or song. Your marriage is a union designed by God, blessed by Christ, and sustained by the working of the Holy Spirit in your lives. Yes, as Christian husband and wife you are meant specifically for each other because you are two "whom God hath joined together."

PRAYER

O God, who hast graven us on the palms of Thy hands and dost always keep us before Thee, we thank Thee for joining us as man and wife. May our union, begun, designed, and directed by Thee, find its purpose and its end in Thee, the only true God, and Jesus Christ, Thy dear Son, our Savior. Amen.

LEAVE AND CLEAVE

Upon entering the marriage relationship and establishing your own home, another relationship comes to an end. The relationship of the bride and groom to their parents is deeply changed. True, a son never ceases to be a son, and a daughter never ceases to be a daughter, but the relationship has changed.

The parental home, which once was the center of love and affection, which once offered more security than any place in the world, which once was a place of multiplying joys and sharing sorrows, has now been supplanted by the newly established home of bride and groom. A young husband cannot think of his parents in exactly the same way he did before. The focal point of his love has changed and now concentrates upon his wife. A young wife cannot feel toward her parents exactly as she did before. Her husband has now become her first love. This is as it should be.

However, Christian newlyweds never cease to honor their fathers and their mothers. They never permit their new love for each other, which by its very nature is different in kind, to make them oblivious to the parental love and concern that, in most cases, has sustained them to the day of their marriage.

This change in relationships, this shifting of affections, is an adjustment which entails real perils for many couples. Count the marriages that know unnecessary discord because the young bride is "tied to her mother's apron strings." Count the marriages that lose their sparkle because he is "a mama's boy." Their number is legion, and they are found in all classes of society.

A Christian should make the adjustment with a minimum of emotional disturbance. He knows that God wants him always to love, honor, and respect his parents. He knows that, humanly speaking, he will never be able to repay his parents for all that they have done for him. But he ought never permit his filial love or his sense of obligation to detract from that love which he has pledged to his spouse.

As an illustration in this matter let us consider Christ in His relationship to the church. He never married, and yet He did have a bride — the church. When Mary, His mother, interfered, although unknowingly, with His services of love to His bride (on the occasion of the twelve-year-old Jesus in the temple, and again at the wedding at Cana), Jesus lovingly but firmly informed her that His first task was to show the way of salvation to a world gripped in sin. He never ceased to love Mary. Even on the cross

He was concerned about her welfare. But first in His life was His bride, the church, those who believe in Him for the forgiveness of their sins.

PRAYER

Dear Savior, whose love transcends all human love and relationships, we are often unwise in the expression of our love. Teach us that our love for Thee ought ever be our first love, that through Thee our love for our spouse may ever remain the purest and primary among our human loves. Grant that as we grow in grace our love for Thee will surpass and enrich all our human relationships. Amen.

AND THEY SHALL BE ONE FLESH

A pastor was once preaching to a group of young people about the place of sex in the life of the Christian. The title of his sermon was, "Who Put the Hex on Sex?" A catchy little phrase, indeed! If we stop to think about it, it soon becomes apparent that these few words get right to the core of the problem quicker than some books that have been written on problems of sex.

Sex is an extremely important and determining factor in the life of every individual. It is not Christian to attempt to hide or ignore the matter of sex. In marriage it is such an ever-present and important factor that the success or failure of the marriage may be determined by the attitude of husband and wife toward it.

Prior to your marriage, by divine wisdom clearly expressed in Holy Scripture, and by the limitations of our society expressed in a hundred different ways, you were told to exercise cautious restraint in matters of sex. In the moment when you were pronounced husband and wife what was before forbidden became permissible within the bounds of propriety. Certain

rights and privileges in the area of sex which are sharply forbidden in the unmarried state become permissible in the married state. This adjustment to the marriage relationship is not easy for everyone.

This is not God's fault. This is not the fault of sex. It is because of the hex. How did the hex come about? As always, it is simply another case of man taking the beautiful things of God and twisting and distorting them into something evil. For example, morphine can be a welcome blessing to a man in pain, or it can be a torturing curse to a man addicted to drugs.

There is nothing wrong in sex itself. God Himself created it and placed it in man. The Bible record is very clear, simple, and beautiful (Genesis 2:24, 25): ". . . and they shall be one flesh. And they were both naked, the man and his wife, and were not ashamed."

This does not mean that God placed no restrictions on sex. In fact, God placed restrictions on everything in life, especially the beautiful things. If they became commonplace they would no longer be beautiful.

May God grant that in your marriage the physical or sex relationship will always be a thing of beauty, always approached without shame or guilt but within the restrictions of God's holy Word. If and when either partner of the marriage momentarily loses this God-given perspective of sex, let him remember that the Savior died for all sins — also the sins against the Sixth Commandment — and ask for forgiveness.

PRAYER

O Lord, our Maker and Redeemer, in fashioning the world and all that is therein Thou didst see it, "and behold, it was very good." For Jesus' sake grant that we in our marriage do not take the good and natural gifts which Thou hast instilled in us and bestowed on us and turn them into something sinful and selfish. Grant that even in our most intimate relationships we live to the glory of Thy holy name. Amen.

A few years ago a great Protestant church body gathered in convention drew up a series of 13 summary statements on "Marriage and Family Life." These statements were to be used as guidelines. Statement number four reads in part: "Husband and wife are called to exercise the power of procreation responsibly before God. This implies planning their parenthood in accordance with their ability to provide for their children and carefully nurture them in fullness of Christian faith and life. The health and welfare of the mother-wife should be a major concern in such decisions. Irresponsible conception of children up to the limit of biological capacity and selfish limitation of the number of children are equally detrimental."

If a heading had been furnished for the 13 statements, there is only one that could have been placed before the above statement, namely, "Birth Control," or "Planned Parenthood," as many prefer to call it.

When it comes to applying this statement to your married life there are yet many questions to be answered. When is the conception of children "irresponsible"? This is a relative thing, and therefore only you two people, as Christian husband and wife, can give the answer that applies in your case. When does the limitation of the number of children become "selfish"? Again, this is a relative thing and only you, as Christian husband and wife, can furnish the answer.

God has given His children a great deal of freedom in certain areas. This is one of them. But freedom does not mean license to do as we please. It means the right to make a choice in accordance with God's will for us. Under freedom we sometimes choose what our sinful nature desires.

If the size of your family is to be determined only by unbridled sex indulgence, or on the other hand only by the selfish thought of how much it will cost in time and money if you do have children, then you will not have learned how to properly use the freedom that God has given you.

As in all things, discuss this matter freely with each other and in your prayers to God. In a multitude of ways He will give you His divine direction.

PRAYER

O Father in heaven, whose family fills both heaven and earth, give us, we pray Thee, in the name of Thy dear Child and our Savior, divine wisdom and direction as we plan our family. Conception and birth, life and death, are in Thy hands. We are tools to be used to fulfill Thy purposes. Make us, in our thoughts, words, and deeds, worthy of this privilege and service. Amen.

THY WIFE SHALL BE AS A FRUITFUL VINE — THY CHILDREN LIKE OLIVE PLANTS ABOUT THY TABLE

This was the psalmist's way of telling what the attitude of the Christian husband and wife is to be toward children. The beautiful picture that he draws is quite a contrast to many present-day attitudes. We have heard parents refer to their children not as olive plants but as tax exemptions, or the unpleasant, inevitable consequences of the marriage relationship.

The Christian husband and wife can take only a very positive attitude towards children. The Christian spouse feels this way not only because reproduction and the care of children is one of the reasons God instituted the holy estate of matrimony. (There was a time when some sections of the Christian church taught that this is the primary, if not the sole, purpose of marriage. This cannot be true because sometimes, contrary to all desires and efforts, marriages remain childless, but they remain marriages nevertheless.) He feels this way because he regards children as a gift of God.

When God permits you to have children, He is honoring you by letting you carry out His continuing creation. Children are, in a very real sense, the crown that God places on the estate of holy matrimony. Down through the ages Christians have always recognized children as a gift of God. They have indicated this in many ways — by the names they bestowed (e. g., Theodore means "gift of God"), by the care they gave their children, and by their efforts, already when the child was at a tender age, to instill in it the blessed truths of the Gospel.

The whole idea of children being a gift of God fits naturally into the scheme of Christian concepts. The greatest gift that God gave was a Child — His own dear Son. That Son in turn gave His life on Calvary. Why? So that, as you will recall from the marriage ritual, "The Lord shall bless thee out of Zion; and thou shalt see the good of Jerusalem all the days of thy life. Yea, thou shalt see thy children's children, and peace upon Israel."

PRAYER

> Dear Father in heaven, our Creator and Preserver, Thou alone art the Giver of every good and perfect gift. In Thy time, and according to Thy will, crown our marriage with the richest of blessings. We speak to Thee about children in the name of Thy Child, our Lord and Savior. Amen.

WEDDED LOVE AND FAITHFULNESS

The lyrics of a popular song tell us that "love and marriage go together like a horse and carriage," that "you can't have one without the other." If only this were true. If it were, we would not have one out of every four marriages ending in the divorce courts.

Too often we come upon marriages — some of them of long standing — that appear to have been drained and emptied of the very last drop of love and affection. The marriage still exists, but the love has long since disappeared. We, of course, wonder what brought this about.

There are countless reasons why marriages fail. Perhaps one of the most frequent is that, unlike the song writer who mistakenly made love and marriage synonymous, there are too many couples who differentiate between love and sex. Are love and sex two different things? Considered from one point of view they are one and the same. From another point of view they are quite different.

In the absolute sense they are different. The best proof of this is that all normal adults feel the strong biological urge that we call sex, but not all experience love in the high sense in which we are using the word. Sex is a biological function — a strong instinctual drive — while love is an emotional experience. Love is not a part of man's built-in equipment, but sex is. Sex can be, and often is, casual about its object; love cannot be casual about its object. One is a physical experience, the other an emotional.

In another sense love and sex are one and the same thing. This must be the concept and attitude of truly Christian marriage partners. They must have this attitude not only as a safeguard against unfaithfulness, but more so as a guide and mandate in their physical relations with, and approach to, each other. The Christian spouse thinks of sex as a God-given means of expressing love for his marriage partner in a language that transcends words. At the same time he thinks of love as a pleasant restraint that will never permit him to abuse and degrade the sex relationship.

The life of the Christian — and in a special way this applies to the relationship between a young Christian husband and wife — can be pictured in the form of a wheel. In the center of this wheel, serving as the very hub, is Christ, whom to know is to love and in whom the love of God Himself is revealed. The spokes emanating from this hub of Christ (ian) love are man's intellectual, social, economic, physical, and spiritual relationships. They all center in and are governed by Christian love. Sex can no more be torn

28

out of the hub of Christian love without destroying the wheel than can any other phase of human relationships.

PRAYER

O God, who hast in Thy Son, Jesus Christ, revealed to us divine love, teach and enable us, who are united in the fellowship of holy matrimony, to build and nourish our human love in a true harmony of body, mind, and spirit. Amen.

"WHO GIVETH THIS WOMAN
TO BE MARRIED TO THIS MAN?"

There is a portion of the marriage ritual which receives little attention, and often when it is referred to, it is in a joking manner. Have you ever asked why the question, "Who giveth this woman to be married to this man?" is incorporated in the ritual? What is the real meaning and purpose of the question?

Actually it is a symbolic way of expressing a deep and profound truth. When a man and woman marry they become part of an endless chain of life. As products of their parents' marriage, they are linked to the past. As potential parents of future offspring, they are linked to the future.

After the father answers the question, he seats himself in the congregation. What a beautifully symbolic way of saying that one generation is receding from the stage of life, a generation that has reared its children and kept the torch of life burning, to make way for a new and younger generation whose progeny will in turn bring new hope and life to a disturbed world. After the father is seated, the new family occupies the center of the stage. They become the leading characters in the great drama of life.

God has given to each generation the responsibility of new life. When the father gives the bride away, we actually witness the passing of the responsibility from one generation to the next.

The endless chain of life of which you have now become a part should not be broken, or needlessly weakened, by irresponsibility, or indifference, or selfishness.

The Savior Himself is our best example of one who preserved the chain of life. By His death He tied together for us the poles of eternity. By His death and resurrection He mended the broken chain between Almighty God and sinful man. He carried for us the torch of eternal life.

Your generation is now on the stage. Look to the Savior for guidance and direction so that you will, in a way purposeful to God and man, meet your responsibilties.

PRAYER

Dear Savior, from the foundations of the world Thou hast called me to membership in Thy family. By Thy death and resurrection the chain of life which will bring us into the Abiding City has been made strong and sure. Grant that in our generation we will be always aware of our bond to the past and our responsibility to the future. Amen.

EVEN AS CHRIST IS THE HEAD
OF THE CHURCH

Do you recall that portion of the marriage ritual taken from Eph. 5:22, 23 which reads, "Wives, be subject to your husbands as to the Lord. For the husband is the head of the wife as Christ is the Head of the church, His body, and is Himself its Savior"? It is a beautiful passage of Scripture because in it the apostle describes the relationship between Christ and His church, and then he places alongside this picture the relationship between spouses and says that there should be a definite similarity.

There was a time in the history of Christianity — that period when church and theologians spoke of marriage as a yielding to temptation and weakness, and at the same time extolled celibacy — when the significance of this comparison was lost sight of. The more we study the pages of Holy Scripture in order to learn what it has to say about marriage, the more evident it becomes that marriage is not only a divine natural order and a remedy against sin but a state in which the Christian can show how through faith the natural relationships of life can become symbols of Christ's love, trust, and fidelity.

If the Savior had regarded the married state as a sort of "second choice," He most certainly would not have used it to describe His relationship to those for whom He died. He would never have referred to Himself as the Groom, and to His church as the bride.

The Christian bride and groom, by virtue of the comparison which God's Word makes, find themselves brought together in a deep and wonderfully mysterious relationship. It is more than a relationship created by a civil contract, or a social adjustment justified by man's purposes. It is a relationship which finds its very roots and foundation in the purposes of God and the love of God.

PRAYER

> We pray Thee, our Father in heaven, who didst institute marriage, Thy dear Son who blessed it, and Thy Holy Spirit who sanctifies it, to make us ever mindful of the relationship that our marriage symbolizes. The pattern of Thy love for the church is the pattern of our love for each other. May it always be so. Amen.

THE ROLES OF HUSBANDS AND WIVES
IN GOD'S ORDER — I

It was only about a century ago — the era of our great-grandparents — when the problems associated with marriage, the family, and the home were given very little attention. They did not require the extensive study and investigation they are receiving today. Society was not nearly as complex as it is today. The economic role, the social status, the physical responsibility, and the division of labor for husband and wife were all quite clearly defined when compared to the mixed and clouded thinking that we have on these matters today.

In the face of all this confusion we find many husbands and wives quite bewildered about their respective responsibilities and duties in the new family unit they are establishing.

Society may change, but God's Word and human nature do not change. The problem is to apply God's Word to a changing society.

The husband is the head of the wife. This is the natural order which God Himself ordained. The status of women in Western society has been constantly upgraded since the rise of Christianity. This is an inherent feature of Christianity. But it does not change the natural order which God Himself prescribed.

This has nothing to do with "women's rights," or "the equality of women," or "woman suffrage." These all Christians, male and female, favor as long as they are within the framework of the divine order.

When we come upon a married couple where the husband is meek and submissive and completely dominated by an aggressive, loud, authoritarian wife we may jokingly say, "Guess who the boss in that house is!" But down deep we feel bad about the whole situation. We cannot bring ourselves to respect the husband, and we most certainly do not admire the wife. Something is wrong. The divine order has miscarried.

The husband is the head of the wife, not in the sense that his is "the master's voice" in all matters, but in the sense that God has selected him to play a very definite role in the family. He is to give the family strength, stability, security. He is to be the shelter for the other members of the family when the storms of life break. In order to fill this role properly he cannot be dominated by the very people to whom he is supposed to be a symbol of refuge.

The husband is the head of the wife, but he exercises this headship only in love. (Billy Sunday once said, "If you want your wife to be an angel, don't treat her like the devil.") The Christian husband would no more abuse this headship than he would abuse his own body. The understanding Christian wife knows this and finds comfort and wisdom in the divine order.

PRAYER

> O Lord, cause me as a husband to love my wife, "even as Christ also loved the church, and gave Himself for it, that He might sanctify and cleanse it with the washing of water by the Word, that He might present it to Himself a glorious church, not having spot, or wrinkle, or any such thing, but that it should be holy and without blemish."
>
> Help me to love my wife as my own body, for "he that loveth his wife loveth himself. For no man ever yet hated his own flesh, but nourisheth and cherisheth it, even as the Lord the church." Amen.

THE ROLES OF HUSBANDS AND WIVES
IN GOD'S ORDER — II

In the marriage ritual there is a question directed to the bride which reads as follows: "Wilt thou love, honor, cherish, *and obey him,* and keep with him this bond of wedlock holy and unbroken till death you do part?" Some pastors have been requested by brides, on occasion, to omit the word "obey." Apparently these brides felt that that word is too strong and ascribes to the husband, by implication, greater authority than they wished to recognize.

Let's be charitable and say that they made the request because they really had not familiarized themselves with the entire ritual, but permitted themselves the dangerous liberty of tearing a word out of its context and applying their own definition.

What does the Bible say about the position of the wife in the family? The answer is clear and concise — "Therefore as the church is subject unto Christ, so let the wives be unto their own husbands in everything."

Before we begin trying to determine what it means for a wife to be subject to her husband, let us not make the mistake, as is so often done, of overlooking the first phrase in the sentence, namely, "as the church is subject unto Christ."

Was there ever a time when the true church felt that it did not want to be subject to Christ? Was there ever a time when Christ, the Head of the church, ruled and governed His flock like a ruthless tyrant? Has there ever been a time when you, as a Christian, have felt that Christ has dealt with you in a loveless, unjust manner? Has there ever been a time when in obeying Christ you were made to feel like a dog obeying his master? Of course, the answer is no. The whole relationship is one of limitless love and not of tyranny and domination.

When the wife is subject to her husband she is fulfilling a very definite role that God has given her. In the home where the husband represents strength, stability, and security, the wife should supply tenderness, compassion, encouragement, beauty, and understanding. The contributions of both are vitally essential to the establishment of a real home.

When a young man looks for a wife, does he desire the most mannish, self-sufficient, independent woman he can find? Quite the opposite. By nature (the divine order) he wants a woman who is truly feminine, charming, tender, and, in the good sense of the word, dependent. On the other hand, when a young lady is looking for a husband, does she seek out the most submissive, meek, unadventurous and dependent man she can find? Just the opposite. By nature (the divine order) she desires a husband who is masculine and virile, confident and courageous, and even adventurous and bold — someone to cling to in adversity.

In a truly Christian family the subject of "who is the head of the family?" never comes up. What should come up in the heart and mind of each of you regularly is this question — "Am I fulfilling the wonderful and unique role that God according to His divine order has given me as a husband (wife)?" If both of you can answer this question in the affirmative, you will have no trouble with the husband abusing his headship or with the wife complaining about her position as subject.

PRAYER

O Lord, cause me as a wife to submit myself "unto my own husband as unto the Lord. For the husband is the head of the wife, even as Christ is the Head of the church; and He is the Savior of the body. Therefore, as the church is subject unto Christ," so let me be unto my own husband in everything. Amen.

YOUR MUTUAL CONSENT
SINCERELY AND FREELY GIVEN

When you spoke your marriage vows to God and to each other before witnesses, you were giving yourselves to each other as of that day and for all the days to come. Prior to that time, or to your engagement, you had no claim upon each other and you imposed no standards upon each other. Perhaps you know little or nothing about the romance (if there was any) that was in the life of your spouse before you were acquainted. If it has not concerned you until this time, why start inquiring now? If it has concerned you, it's best to forget about it.

Frequently in newspaper columns generally known as "advice to the lovelorn" we read about a young husband or wife who is so persistent in digging into the antemarital past that the marriage partner, in a moment of intimacy, and having the promise that "nothing will matter," tells all. The results are always painful and unpleasant. How can they be otherwise?

A husband or wife is not required either by God or man to reveal to the spouse all experiences, both good and bad, of premarital days. However, if past sins are revealed, there is the Christian duty of forgiveness. This will be easier if we remember that we are *all* sinners in desperate need of forgiveness.

While it is true that it is not advisable for husband and wife to withold any great secrets from each other, it is also true that you accepted each other for what you were on the day of your marriage. Even if husband and wife do share with each other their personal, intimate experiences before marriage, they must, as Christians, always guard against sitting in judgment on an incident that took place a long time ago under circumstances that could never be accurately and actually reconstructed.

If the Savior would deal with us this way our lives would be filled with regret and despair and we never would reach heaven. Through the apostle Paul He tells us what our attitude should be — "Forgetting what lies behind and straining forward to what lies ahead, I press on toward the goal for the prize of the upward call of God in Christ Jesus." (Philippians 3:13, 14)

PRAYER

Grant, O Lord, that the happiness which we now know in our marriage may never be marred or disturbed by the past. By the forgiveness which Thou hast granted to each of us we stand before Thee dressed in the garment of Thy righteousness alone. Amen.

Perhaps one of the most essential ingredients of a happy and satisfying Christian marriage is the element of trust. Husband and wife, if they are ever to find genuine and abiding peace in their marriage, must have implicit trust in each other. You, as a wife, must be convinced that your husband would never take the love and affection that he has promised to you and give it to another woman. The same applies, of course, to you, the husband, in your relationship to your wife. Never should you permit yourself even to suspect that your spouse might be unfaithful.

When Joseph became aware of the fact that the Virgin Mary was to give birth to a child, we do not read that he immediately cast her aside and accused her of adultery. He could well have done this and been faulted by no one. The Holy Record says, "Then Joseph, her husband, being a just man. . . ." Soon a messenger direct from God, in the form of an angel, explained the whole situation to trusting Joseph. What would have been interpreted an offensive and unclean relationship on the part of Mary was soon seen for what it really was — the most beautiful plan that God Himself has devised for man.

The Kinsey reports that have been issued in recent years would indicate that there is a shocking amount of marital infidelity. We would be naive to assume that all husbands are faithful to their wives and that all wives are faithful to their husbands. This would be a gross underestimation of the devil, the world, and our own flesh.

However, as a Christian husband or wife, you must assume that it cannot happen to your spouse. It can happen to you as an individual, and therefore you must ever guard against it, but never let it enter your mind that it could happen to your spouse. We show trust in each other as husband and wife, not by keeping a constant vigil on each other, not by questioning the faithfulness of each other, but by doing just the opposite — by placing unwavering confidence in the exclusiveness of each other's love.

Christian marriages are born in and flourish in the virtue of mutual trust. They soon smother and die when covered by the blanket of suspicion.

PRAYER

Dear Savior, who alone hast never violated a trust, grant that the trust and the confidence we now have in each other may never know doubt or change. As we now give ourselves wholly and completely to each other, may we always keep ourselves wholly and completely for each other. Amen.

"CLOTHE YOURSELVES, ALL OF YOU, WITH HUMILITY TOWARD ONE ANOTHER." 1 Peter 5:5

The days of courtship that lead up to marriage are invaluable. They serve as a preparatory period for the lifelong marriage relationship that lies ahead. Yet, in a sense, they constitute a period of artificial living in the story of our lives.

The young man is always on his best behavior as he courts his future wife. He is courteous, neat, prompt, patient. He is doing everything in his power to make a good impression, to be liked. In many cases he does everything but be himself.

The young lady also comes in for her share of artificial behavior. She is absolutely meticulous about her dress. She strives always to say the right thing at the right time. She does everything to be as charming as possible. Many times she also does everything but be herself.

Artificiality can, and often does, lead to false pride. Sometimes, the artificiality and false pride carry over from the days of courtship to the days of marriage.

Jesus, through His holy writer says, "Clothe yourselves, all of you, with humility toward one another."

The Savior is here not telling us that when a couple is married they need no longer give attention to personal appearance — that they should cease trying to be charming — that they should leave off striving for the social virtues. He does tell us, however, that in the Christian life — and it applies especially to the Christian married life — there is no place for artificiality and pride.

The Christian spouse loves his mate not only because of her fine attributes and virtues, but also because of her faults and weaknesses. The Christian bride or bridegroom does not hesitate to mention a weakness or a shortcoming to his or her spouse, and such gentle reminders should be taken in the right spirit.

Christian marriage partners should be humble, honest, and open toward each other. This is one of the great blessings of marriage.

This is one of the reasons true believers, real members of the body of Christ, are relaxed, comfortable, and happy in the presence of Christ, the Bridegroom. There is no attempt at deception. Sins are brought out in the open and confessed. Forgiveness is received, and He who hates the sin ever and always shows His love for the sinner.

Clothe yourselves with humility toward each

other. It will make your marriage much more comfortable.

PRAYER

Dear Lord, whose humility extended even to death and the grave in order that we might have life and eternity, remove from us all artificiality and pride in our relationship as husband and wife. May our greatest pride be Thy presence as a guest in our home. Amen.

God Himself made the statement that heads this page. He directed it to Eve. The statement was probably used in your marriage ritual when the officiant introduced them with these words, "Hear also the cross which by reason of sin God hath laid upon this estate."

The estate of holy matrimony is not immune to sin. It would be well for you at this early period in your married life to discuss what your course will be when sins are committed, and what your strength will be when the consequences of the sins arrive.

We know how to handle sins in our lives, thanks to our gracious and loving Savior, Jesus Christ. It is the same for all people, married or single. First, we confess them to our God. (We may also confess to man. Husband and wife may well serve each other in the capacity of confessor and confessee). Second, we ask for forgiveness. Third, we determine to do our utmost, with the help of God, not to fall into the same sin again.

Now, if we believe this, the sin so handled is gone forever — washed away by the blood of the Lamb. The consequence, however, may remain and have to be endured. For example, the sin of reckless driving which led to an accident may be forgiven, but the physical injury which resulted may endure for a lifetime. Where do we find the strength, understanding, and patience to bear such crosses as this if they occur in our lives? We, of course, "lift up our eyes unto the hills from whence cometh our help." The Lord never gives us a burden greater than we can bear. If the burden is heavy, He gives us added strength. Abraham knew this. Moses knew it. David knew it. Peter knew it. Paul knew it. Yes, all the hosts of saints that have gone before knew it. They went to the hill of God's strength for their help. Follow in the footsteps of the saints.

You can share this divine strength with one another and so build one another up in the faith. As fellow redeemed by Christ, you constantly hold up each other's hands by sharing the help that you receive at God's holy hill. Just as you like to hear your spouse tell you often that he (she) loves you, so also your spouse as a Christian never tires of hearing of the love of God. Reassure each other of God's love.

PRAYER

> Chief of sinners though I be,
> Jesus shed His blood for me;
> Died that I might live on high,
> Lived that I might never die.
> As the branch is to the vine,
> I am His, and He is mine. Amen.

FOR BETTER, FOR WORSE

A man in his seventies went to the doctor for a physical examination. At the conclusion of the examination the doctor pronounced him physically well and healthy and inquired about the rules of health he followed in order to maintain his physical fitness.

The aged gentleman replied, "when my wife and I were married more than fifty years ago, we agreed that whenever she lost her temper because of any fault in me she would keep quiet, and that whenever I would lose my temper because of any fault in her I would take a walk. Perhaps my good health can be attributed to the fact that for more than fifty years I have lived pretty much of an outdoor life."

Yes, it makes us chuckle, but underneath lies the sad reality that here were two people that never accepted their spouses for what they really were. For more than half a century they unsuccessfully tried to reform and refashion each other's personalities. The project of "making a new man" or "making a new woman" of your spouse seldom meets with success. Even if it does succeed, it is often questionable if the refashioned personality is an improvement on the original.

There is a wise old saying that reads, "the time to keep both eyes open is before marriage, and the time to keep one eye closed is after marriage." Each must learn to accept the other for what he is. In a sense the following well-known prayer is most appropriate when evaluating your spouse: "God grant me the serenity to accept the things I cannot change, the courage to change the things I can, and the wisdom to know the difference."

Even as sinful man is refashioned and remade to the point where he "grows in grace," not by the stinging whip and cutting sword of God's Law, but rather by the love of God as he comes to know it in Jesus Christ, so also the inadequate spouse, if he must be fault-finding, but rather by loving patience and tender understanding.

PRAYER

> Dear Savior, even as I have Your divine and eternal love in spite of my many sins and weaknesses, so may my love for my spouse be unaffected by sins and weaknesses. If I too often see the mote in my spouse's eye, remind me of the beam in my own eye. Even as there is always forgiveness with Thee, so may we always find forgiveness in each other. Amen.

"IN HONESTY AND INDUSTRY
TO PROVIDE FOR EACH OTHER"

As Christian husband and wife you did not enter the estate of holy matrimony for reasons of financial gain. The glib saying "it's just as easy to love them if they are rich" may be true, but the "rich" part should be only incidental and never the motivating force behind a marriage.

Nevertheless, money and the way in which it is handled, is an important factor in every marriage. If either of the marriage partners is irresponsible in this area, the billows of the sea of matrimony can become dangerously tempestuous. An old adage says, "when the wolf is at the door, love flies out the window." Fortunately the adage is only an adage and not at all descriptive of what happens in a truly Christian marriage when the wolf is at the door. Financial problems, as all problems, can strengthen a marriage by bringing husband and wife together in a common cause. Here is a problem that can be solved only by co-operation, understanding, and perseverance.

Most frequently difficulties arise in the family finances when there is too great a disparity in the financial backgrounds of the marriage partners. Two people, even husband and wife, with different sets of financial values, and different attitudes toward money, can very readily disagree on how money is to be used. What one regards as a luxury, the other may consider a necessity.

In order to avoid difficulties in the administration of the family funds, some very basic concepts should be resolved upon at the very beginning of the marriage. First, husband and wife should constantly remind themselves that all their material possessions, whether in abundance or otherwise, really belong to God. We are merely stewards. This starting point is most important.

Second, a plan or budget for the spending and saving of the family income should be mutually decided upon. Each plan or budget must be tailored to the needs of the respective couple.

Third, the responsibility of handling the finances should be equally shared. While one does the actual handling of the funds, this does not mean that the other has no part in it, is never apprised of what is going on, or is made to feel financially dependent on the other for the most trivial things involving finances.

Achan's wedge of gold has broken many marriages asunder. The Savior, during His public ministry never permitted riches, pleasure, or fame to interfere with the expression of His love for us. May you never permit your love for each other to be threatened or stifled by money, but rather use it as a means of expressing your love for each other.

PRAYER

Lord, the eyes of all wait upon Thee. Thou openest Thy hands and satisfiest the desire of every living thing. May we always use Thy bounty to show our love for Thee and each other. Amen.

LOVE BEARS ALL THINGS

A brief excerpt from the diary of a Christian wife and mother appeared as follows: "Nov. 29. Mary and Joe (little daughter and son), struggling with a piano duet, remind me of the early years of a marriage. Takes a lot of practice, patience, and willingness to overlook the partner's mistakes before you can make beautiful music together. Harmony doesn't come without effort."

If someone would ask you to supply in a few words the most essential ingredients that are required to establish a Christian marriage and a God-pleasing family life, you would most likely, sooner or later, come up with these Christian virtues — patience, kindness, unselfishness. Notice how each of these virtues partakes of the others. Is it possible for a person to be truly patient and yet unkind and selfish? Or is it possible for one to be filled with human kindness and at the same time be impatient and selfish?

Notice further that each of the three virtues, if truly possessed and practiced, requires a forgetting or divesting of one's self. Egocentricity — complete occupation with one's self and problems — cannot live under the same roof with patience, kindness, and unselfishness. To use the language of the marriage counselor, they are "incompatible." Egocentricity can, and often does, bring about incompatibility in marriage.

The duet that produces the perfect marriage requires perfect tempo, perfect rhythm, perfect touch, perfect expression. Your spouse does not possess all these qualities — nor do you. However, if you will see each other with the eye of patience, hear each other with the ear of kindness, and know each other with the touch of unselfishness, you will be satisfied and happy in your marriage.

All of the things we have said here the apostle Paul expresses most beautifully (1 Cor. 13:4-7). "Love is patient and kind; love is not jealous or boastful; it is not arrogant or rude. Love does not insist on its own way; it is not irritable or resentful; it does not rejoice at wrong, but rejoices in the right. Love bears all things, hopes all things, endures all things."

Yes, the apostle Paul said it beautifully, and the Savior lived it perfectly — in our stead.

PRAYER

Dear Savior, give us, we pray Thee, in our marriage an abundant measure of Thy perfect love. Only then will we have the patience, kindness, and unselfishness so necessary for a happy and successful marriage. When our love fails and we become intolerant of the weaknesses of the other, turn us to Thee for forgiveness and strength. Amen.

What are the things which pertain to God? In the theological sense, all things pertain to God. Some Christian writers have put it in this way. God has full claim on our time, talents, and treasure. The way in which we respond to this claim and place our time, talents, and treasure at His disposal is called "stewardship." Every Christian is a steward (one who acts as an administrator of property for another) whether he wants to be or not. The question is, is he a good steward or a bad steward, does he practice good stewardship or bad stewardship? Furthermore, good stewardship is the responsibility of every Christian, whether he be married or single, young or old.

For reasons which are more imagined than real, good stewardship often breaks down in the initial stages of marriage. New relationships, new duties, new responsibilities tend to make the young couple forget that they as individuals and as a couple are a force to be used by God and not simply humans engaged in self-preservation and self-indulgence.

If God has given either of you talents as teachers, leaders, musicians, organizers, etc., then even the busy schedule of newly married life does not excuse you from placing these talents at His disposal.

The all-knowing Lord is aware that the young husband is much occupied in carving out a career in a hard, cold, competitive world. For the spiritual refreshment that he so much needs, there is only one place to find abundant supply, namely, in the service of his God and his fellow man. He may have to make a choice between the church choir and the country club, between the service club and the Sunday school, between the poker party and parish program.

The all-knowing Lord is aware that the young wife, like Martha, "is troubled about many things" in the establishment of her new home.

Time and again in the New Testament the Savior warned those who desired real discipleship not to become too encumbered with the affairs of this world. We pray the same thing for each married couple when we ask that they "pray for and encourage each other in the things which pertain to God."

PRAYER

> O God of mercy, God of might,
> In love and pity infinite,
> Teach us, as ever in Thy sight,
> To live our life to Thee.
> And may Thy Holy Spirit move
> All those who live to live in love
> Till Thou shalt greet in heaven above
> All those who live to Thee. Amen.

"TO PRAY FOR AND ENCOURAGE
EACH OTHER" — II

Our time, talents, and treasure are really possessions of God placed in our care to be used in the service of God and man.

Let us direct our attention specifically to the third "T" — treasure. Let us become even more specific in our thinking and consider how the material possessions that God has given us are to be used in His service — the stewardship of money.

You were married in God's house. He was a guest at your wedding. Then and now you feel that you want Him always as a guest in your home. In addition to the blessing that He has given you in each other, there was, as is the custom, a generous outpouring of gifts at your wedding. Also, one or both of you are gainfully employed.

Now, as children of a completely unselfish God that bought you back at a tremendous price, you must together decide what portion of your material blessings you will return to Him. The pattern you set now, in the early days of your marriage, will have an immeasurable effect on the spiritual tone and atmosphere of your home.

Many Christians believe that the wise and Scriptural way to arrive at the amount that is to be returned to God through the church and other deserving agencies is to give on a percentage basis. This is your way of saying to God, "When the windows of heaven open and rain down upon us abundant blessings, we want to return them to You in abundance. In the event lean years come upon us, we know that You will be pleased with a less abundant offering."

In a general way our income tax system is predicated on a percentage basis — the more you make, the more you pay. Most people feel that as long as we have to have an income tax, this system is as equitable as any. One great difference between the percentage approach in income tax and the percentage approach in Christian stewardship of money is that the first is compulsory and the latter is completely voluntary.

The good stewardship of money for your church and your Lord requires a certain amount of self-imposed discipline and sacrifice.

There will never be a more opportune time in your lives for you as husband and wife to accept the challenge of the Lord when He says "Bring ye all the tithes into the storehouse, that there may be meat in Mine house, and prove Me now herewith, saith the

59

Lord of hosts, if I will not open you the windows of heaven and pour you out a blessing that there shall not be room enough to receive it." (Malachi 3:10)

PRAYER

> We give Thee but Thine own,
> Whate'er the gift may be;
> All that we have is Thine alone,
> A trust, O Lord, from Thee.
>
> May we Thy bounties thus
> As stewards true receive
> And gladly, as Thou blessest us,
> To Thee our first fruits give! Amen.

"THAT THEY MAY MAKE THEIR HOME
AND THEIR HEARTS
THY DWELLING PLACE"

William Lyon Phelps, a great teacher, once said, "Since the greatest of all arts is the art of living together, and since the highest and most permanent values depend upon it, and since the way to practice this art successfully lies through character, the all-important question is how to obtain character. The surest way is through religion in the home."

"Religion in the home" can mean many things. The Holy Bible is as much a fixture in many American homes as the mail-order catalog. Often, in fact, the two are kept in the same bookcase and enjoy a life of undisturbed quiet under the same cover of dust. This could be regarded as having religious literature in the home, but it is not "religion in the home" in the true sense of the word.

In other homes, as a matter of perfunctory routine, a prayer is spoken at the beginning and end of every meal. Sometimes this becomes so perfunctory that we find people using the prayer intended for the conclusion of the meal at the beginning and vice versa.

After the first few phrases have been intoned, there is an embarrassed silence and then, after sheepish grins, the proper prayer is spoken. It is in such moments that, in a most forceful way, we are brought to the startling realization that even religion can become a matter of habit.

"Religion in the home," if it has its proper place, never becomes a matter of habit. While its outward expression very often does settle into a pattern of regularity (e. g., prayers on rising and retiring, before and after meals), the pattern itself should never be permitted to take the place of genuine religious experience and spiritual expression.

The religion in your home is going to be only as deep and true as the religion in your heart. Here is where husband and wife can truly support and strengthen each other. In an uninhibited way they can, and should, speak to each other about spiritual matters. They should share their thoughts about Christ, about sin and forgiveness.

PRAYER

> Oh, blest the house, whate'er befall,
> Where Jesus Christ is all in all!
> Yea, if He were not dwelling there,
> How dark and poor and void it were!
>
> Oh, blest that house where faith ye find
> And all within have set their mind
> To trust their God and serve Him still
> And do in all His holy will!

GOD BLESSES THOSE WHO TRUST IN HIM

Centuries ago a king, plagued by many worries, harassed on every side, called his wise men together. He asked them to invent a motto, a few magic words that would help him in time of trial or distress. It must be brief enough to be engraved on a ring, he said, so that he could have it always before his eyes. It must be appropriate to every situation.

The wise men thought and thought and finally came to the king with their magic words. They were words for every change or chance of fortune . . . words to fit every situation, bad or good . . . words to ease the heart and mind in every circumstance. The motto they furnished the king was: *This, Too, Shall Pass Away*.

Think about these words for a moment and you will have to admit that they are wise and true and endlessly enduring. Paul H. Hayne, inspired by the phrase, wrote a poem bearing the same title. The poem is said to have furnished power and inspiration to countless thousands.

However, for the Christian the motto is not the

complete story. There is in it, if you listen carefully, a steady undertone of futility. Is life nothing more than just a series of things or incidents "passing away"? To the Christian it is infinitely more.

This motto may have been satisfactory to a pagan king, but it was only because he knew of nothing better. Christians know of something better. Something furnished, not to a king, but by a King — the King of Glory.

One day the Lord's disciples were sharing with Him a few precious moments of private, intimate discussion. They wanted to know when He would return and what the signs of His return would be. In the course of the conversation He told them: "Heaven and earth shall pass away, but My words shall not pass away." (Matthew 24:35)

This is by far the better motto for your marriage, because it incorporates not only the wisdom of the wise men but the promises of Almighty God.

PRAYER

O Lord God, be Thou "our refuge and strength, a very present help in trouble." Then we "will not . . . fear though the earth be removed and though the mountains be carried into the midst of the sea." Keep us ever mindful that Thou art in the midst of "the city of God, the holy place of Thy tabernacles," and that "she shall not be moved" even though "the heathen rage." Help us always to realize that Thou, "the God of Jacob" art "our refuge." Amen. (Cf. Psalm 46)

BUILDING ON A ROCK OR ON SAND
Matthew 7:24-27

In the seventh chapter of the Gospel According to St. Matthew Jesus tells the story of two men, one wise and one foolish. The wise man, He says, is the one who built his house on a rock, and the foolish one is the man who built his house on sand.

As you now enter upon the lifelong project of establishing a family and building house and a home, you can be either wise or foolish, depending on the foundation you select for the undergirding of your home.

If you build your house on sand, the preparation for the building is not nearly as arduous and the erection time is not nearly as long. By that we mean that if both of you direct all of your time and energies toward the acquiring of material things — a beautiful house, a shiny new car, and the latest styles in clothes, the appearance that you will give to the world will be one of success and achievement. But what will happen to your house if the rains of discontent, the floods of sickness, and the winds of adversity blow against it? The costly furniture, the shiny new car, and the stylish clothes will be too weak a foundation to sustain you.

Unless you build your marriage on a rock — and this can be done only by directing your time and energies to those values that are lasting and real — it is possible that your marriage may not weather the storms of life.

What are some of the stones that go into the foundation of a marriage that is solid as a rock? The first stone that must be laid is that of spirituality. Unless each of you has a clear understanding of your relationship with Jesus Christ, you will find your relationship with each other difficult. The first commandment of the Decalog, "Thou shalt have no other gods before Me," is also the first commandment for a successful marriage. The material things in marriage are not evil or sand in themselves, but they can become so when not put in their proper place. What is their proper place? Jesus made it very clear when He said, "Seek ye first the kingdom of God and His righteousness, and all these things shall be added unto you."

A second stone that must be laid is that of unselfish love — the kind of love that is forever seeking what it might give rather than what it might receive.

In the New Testament the apostle Paul uses three different Greek words meaning love. They differ not in degree, but in kind. The first is erotic or romantic love (self-satisfying). There is some of this in your marriage, and you need not be ashamed of it. But it is only sand and not rock. Second is the type of love that two people, very intimate and close, have for each other's person and welfare (love that is returned). There should be much of this in your marriage. But it is not the rock substance needed for the foundation. Third is the deep, genuine, spiritual affection that cannot help but give and serve and even suffer in exercising itself. It does all this without looking for anything good or lovable in the object of its love. The perfect example of this — one to which you can never attain, but for which, as husband and wife, you should always strive — is the love that drove the Savior relentlessly to the cross.

Build your marriage on these foundation stones, and you will never have to fear the floods or rain or winds of misfortune.

PRAYER

Dear Lord, help us realize the truth of the following lines:

How firm a foundation, ye saints of the Lord,
Is laid for your faith in His excellent Word!
What more can He say than to you He hath said
Who unto the Savior for refuge have fled?

"HEIRS TOGETHER OF THE GRACE
OF LIFE."   1 Peter 3:7

Sir Hugh Walpole said it. "The most wonderful of all things in life, I believe, is the discovery of another human being with whom one's relationship has a glowing depth, beauty, and joy as the years increase. The inner progressiveness of love between two human beings is a most marvelous thing; it cannot be found by looking for it or by passionately wishing for it. It is a sort of divine accident."

We do not in any way wish to distort the beautiful thought so ably expressed by this great man of letters, but look carefully at the last sentence. Is there such a thing as a divine accident? Is it just an accident that God has brought you together as man and wife? Is it just an accident that the family you will raise and the home you will establish as Christian husband and wife will serve as a dwelling place for the Triune God with all His blessings? Is it just an accident that the joy you have known in each other, and will continue to know, is far more than you ever deserved?

If these be accidents, divine or otherwise, then they have been carefully arranged by One who has even greater plans in store for you. You are to be "heirs together of the grace of life." At this point now, even in the midst of all the joy and happiness that your marriage has brought, you must try to sit back and see the whole arrangement for what it really is. Your marriage in the eyes of God is a brief period of time, a mere "moment between sun and frost," in the long pilgrimage that you are making between the poles of eternity. He claimed you as His own from the foundations of the world, and it is just a matter of time until you will be with Him in the Abiding City.

But a pilgrimage by its very nature is a difficult journey. To lighten the burden, to strengthen the body, to refresh the spirit, He has given you to each other as partners on the way. There will be times when one will be weak and the other strong, but there will never be a time when you will not need each other.

The same Lord loves each of you with the same limitless love and stands ready to help you fill your role as husband and wife. He is so sure that your marriage will be filled with blessings that He has made you "heirs together of the grace of life." Trust in Him.

PRAYER

Dear Savior, who art the same yesterday, today, and forever, and with whom a thousand years is but a moment in time, raise our sights so that we may see beyond the immediate to the eternal and lasting. Cause us always to remember that our marriage was designed by Thee, is to be lived in Thy presence, and reaches its culmination only at the marriage feast of the Lamb. To this high and noble destiny, help us, O God, to direct each other. Amen.

PRAYERS FOR NEWLYWEDS

Almighty God, who didst create man and woman, and didst join them together in marriage, thereby signifying the mystery of the union between Thy Son Jesus Christ and His Bride, the church: we beseech Thine infinite goodness, let not this Thy blessed work and ordinance be set aside or brought to naught, but graciously protect and preserve it. Especially let Thy blessing rest upon us Thy servants; so rule us by Thy Holy Spirit that we may live together to Thy glory and to our own welfare in this life and in that which is to come. Keep us in Thy favor, and bring us unto everlasting life; through Jesus Christ, our Lord. Amen.

Lord, our God, our Helper and our Comforter in time and in eternity, graciously look upon us Thy servants, who according to Thy holy ordinance have entered the covenant of wedded love and troth. Do Thou bless us, and so guide us by Thy Holy Spirit that in all things Thy good and gracious will may be done in us. May we let the Word of Christ dwell in us richly, and do Thou make our home and our hearts

Thy dwelling place. Grant that our souls be united in Christ Jesus unto one mind by love, and may our mutual true affection never know doubt or change. Do Thou bless us in each other, and enable us in wisdom and meekness to bear with patience each other's infirmities. Prosper the work of our hands, and crown our lives with Thy loving-kindness and tender mercies. Let even our crosses and afflictions yield us the peaceable fruit of righteousness as an abiding blessing, and teach us in everything by prayer and supplication with thanksgiving to make our requests known unto Thee. And when in steadfast faith we have finished our pilgrimage on earth, give us a dwelling place with Thee in heavenly joy; for the sake of Jesus Christ, Thy Son, our Lord. Amen.